Trials on Purpose: Sculpted by Suffering, Strengthened by His Spirit

Schniece M. Lambert

Trials on Purpose

Copyright © 2025 Schniece M. Lambert
All rights reserved.

All rights reserved. No part of this publication may be reproduced, stored in a retrieval system, or transmitted in any form or by any means-for example, electronic, photocopy, recording-without the prior written permission of the publisher. The only exceptions are brief quotations in printed reviews.
For information about custom editions, special sales, premium and bulk purchases, please contact:
authorschniece@gmail.com
www.rise2write.com
Publisher: Rise2Write Publishing LLC

"But He knows the way that I take; when He has tested me, I shall come forth as gold." *(Job 23:10 NKJV)*

Trials on Purpose

DEDICATION

To the One who has never let go of my hand, Jesus, You are the author of this offering. Without You, I would have been lost and consumed by the fire. But with You, I discovered the oil within it. This book represents just a portion of my alabaster jar, shattered at Your feet. Be glorified in every word and be visible through every scar. This is all for You.

To my children, thank you, God, for choosing me to steward your lives. You all are my why; you are the ink between every line and the pause between every prayer. May you always know that your life is not an accident but a divine assignment. I thank you for your patience, understanding, and love during the most turbulent times in our lives. You carry legacy in your blood, purpose in your bones, and heaven's handprint on your heart. If you ever forget who you are, come back to these pages and remember who you were created to be.

To my parents, I thank God for the blessing of calling you Mom and Dad. I thank you for planting seeds that you didn't always get to see bloom. Your prayers watered the ground I now stand on. Your sacrifices became the soil from which this voice has risen. I honor the late nights, the quiet intercessions, and the unseen faithfulness. Because of your foundation, I was able to rise. To those who walked with me in silence, through storms, and in sacred friendship, thank you for believing in the call when I barely believed in myself. For holding space when I was unraveling, and for speaking life when all I could hear was doubt. You may never know how your "yes" helped unlock mine.

To every mentor, spiritual mother and father, encourager, and co-laborer, thank you for investing in, challenging, correcting, and supporting me. You showed me what grace looks like in action. You helped me understand that brokenness isn't a disqualifier; it's a doorway.

Table of Contents

Introduction ix

Prologue: The Question in the Fire 1

Chapter One: The Fire That Forms Us 5

Chapter Two: Set Apart to See 11

Chapter Three: Humbled for Glory 19

Chapter Four: The Posture of Prayer: Accessing Divine Power in the Midst of Trials 31

Chapter Five: A People of Purpose 45

Chapter Six: The Process 55

Chapter Seven: The War You Didn't See Coming .. 61

Chapter Eight: Warfare Isn't Proof God Left, It's Proof You're Advancing 67

Chapter Nine: You Can't Walk in Public Authority Without Private Crushing 73

Chapter Ten: The Restoration 81

Readers Reflection 87

50 Affirmations for your Soul 91

Final Prayers: God, Use My Trials for Your Glory . 95

Prayer of Salvation 99

ABOUT THE AUTHOR 101

Trials on Purpose

Introduction

Nobody volunteers for pain. We don't wake up asking God for heartbreak, betrayal, storms, loss, trials, and wilderness seasons. Many of us ask for blessings, we ask for favor, we ask for open doors, and we ask for a breakthrough. But what if the blessing is hidden in the breaking? What if the fire you tried to escape was the furnace where your calling was forged?

I found out trials don't come to destroy you, they come to define you. To refine what's real, to strip away what's false, and to provoke the kind of growth that only pressure can produce. Believe it or not, contrary to what culture tells us, purpose isn't birthed in comfort. It is birthed in the crushing. In the dark rooms, in the sleepless nights, in the gut-wrenching, clenched teeth and teary-eyed "God, where are You?" prayers. Unfortunately, you don't get oil without pressing, you don't get gold without fire, and you don't get to destiny without some level of devastation. Here's what they didn't tell you in the valley: the valley isn't punishment, it is preparation. God is not trying to break you down; He is actually building you up. Every tear you cried has been counted. Every loss you suffered, guess what, it has been measured. Every betrayal you have endured has been repurposed. Because your pain is not random, it's prophetic. I've learned that there is an assignment behind every crushing, a blueprint behind every delay, and a promise woven into every wound. Even when the enemy thought he would finish you and you thought it would take you out, God was using it to establish you.

This book is a reckoning, a holy confrontation with the lie that God is only present in the good days. Family, the truth is, He is most present when you feel the most forsaken.

So, if you're walking through the fire right now, or trying to find your way out of the ashes, don't run; press in. Press into His presence and let heaven reframe what has hurt you. I promise you won't just survive the storm this time; you'll understand why it came and embrace it. This is your awakening, this is "Trials on Purpose: Sculpted by Suffering, Strengthened by His Spirit."

Trials on Purpose

Prologue: The Question in the Fire

There comes a quiet, trembling, yet unbearably loud moment, when you look back over the landscape of your life and wonder: *Was this pain punishment... or purpose?*

Was God still with me when everything fell apart?

Was He the One who allowed it all?

I have walked through valleys so shadowed that I doubted if light would ever return. I've sat in silence and soaked in tears when no one else could see. I have asked and begged God for answers: *"Why me?" "Why now?" "What did I do to deserve this?"*

Perhaps, like me, you have also been there. Standing in the aftermath of what once was, from shattered friendships, finances crumbled, health fading, abuse, homelessness, divorce, death of two children, failed relationships, being lied on, no one to turn to, all the while my faith was flickering.

That is when the enemy's whisper begins…

"Maybe God is angry."

"Maybe I'm being punished."

"Maybe this is payback for my past."

"Maybe there is no reason to live"

But then, amid the storms, tests, and trials, when I began to dissect the Word for myself, not for a sermon, not for show, but for survival, I discovered something unexpected: hope, love, truth, protection, and purpose. The Lord whispered through the noise and chaos, not with condemnation but with compassion. *"For I know the plans I have for you, declares the Lord, plans to prosper you and not to harm you, plans to give you hope and a future."* (Jeremiah 29:11). This book is a snippet of my testimony, not about how perfect I became, but about how faithful my God really is.

It serves as both a mirror and a window, inviting you to see your reflection and your redemption in the midst of the trial. Family, your trials are not random; they are refined, designed, and divinely purposed.

Trials on Purpose

Chapter One: The Fire That Forms Us

"For whom the Lord loves He chastens…" (Hebrews 12:6)

Trials on Purpose

Trials on Purpose

The first truth I had to confront was this: God deals with us as sons. For what son is there whom a father does not chasten? If you are without chastening, of which all have become partakers, then you are illegitimate and not sons. God allows the fire not to burn us, but to build us. Holiness is not born in comfort; it is shaped in the flames of fire. To be holy is to be set apart, carved out from among the common, and disengaged from the ordinary. It is to bear the mark of heaven in a world that glorifies sin. And yet, how often do we resist this refining?

We crave the crown but run from the crucible. Holiness isn't a suggestion, it is a summons. *"Be holy, for I the Lord your God am holy." (Leviticus 19:2)*

It is a divine call to be different, to be light in darkness, to be salt in blandness, and to be alive when everything around you feels lifeless. God allows the trial, not to destroy you, but to draw out what He placed within you before the foundations of the world. When I reflect on the deepest valleys I've walked through, I now see them as sacred places, altars of transformation. The trial was the chisel, sculpting away at old patterns, habits, and belief systems. The suffering was the song; this is where I learned to worship like never before with my own melody. Then the breaking was the beginning, where heaven began to dig deep into the wells of my soul. We are not disqualified by our wounds; we are refined by them.

What once seemed like abandonment, I now perceive as alignment. What once felt like punishment, I now understand as preparation. Not to shame you, but to shape you, position you, and anoint you. He corrects you because He calls you. He disciplines you because He delights in you. The weight of wrath is never meant to destroy you; you are being crafted by the hands of the master Craftsman.

God is not cruel; He is careful. His fire doesn't destroy gold; it reveals it. That's why confident people like me don't walk with arrogance; they walk with a limp. I have wrestled in the dark, I have wept on the threshing floor, and I had everything stripped away until all that was left was God, and somehow, that was enough. Holiness isn't about image; it's about intimacy. It is not a mask you wear; it's a life you live when no one is watching but God.

Family, there is no shortcut; there is no way around the fire. Remember, Jesus is always in the furnace with you. The refining is not your ruin; it's your reminder that you are not common; you are not leftover clay in the hands of the Potter. So don't resist the fire; let it do its holy work. Let it burn away what you were never meant to carry. Let it consume the lies you agreed with. Let it purify the places where compromise once resided. Let it awaken a hunger for righteousness that no platform, applause, or performance could ever satisfy.

The fire that burns today is forming the vessel that will carry glory tomorrow. When you emerge, because you will, you will possess a purity the world cannot replicate and a power that hell cannot counterfeit. You will walk with a clarity that only the crushing can bring, and you will speak with boldness and authority born from affliction. You will understand that holiness is not for the few; it's the inheritance of the yielded. So, if you find yourself in the fire, take heart, it's not evidence that you're forsaken. It is proof that you're being shaped, and on the other side of this, you won't just survive; your light will shine brighter than before, and you will gain access to realms that were once prohibited to you.

Chapter Two: Set Apart to See

"Get out of your country, From your family and from your father's house, To a land that I will show you." (Genesis 12:1)

Trials on Purpose

Sanctification is the slow, sacred work of separation. I had to leave what was comfortable to discover what was eternal. Familiarity had dulled my faith. I had become too cozy with mediocrity, too content with having just enough. God called me away from everything and everyone I knew and relied on. He stripped me of the familiar to allow me to tap into the faith to follow Him. Like Abraham, I didn't have the whole map, only the next step. Honestly, I didn't want to go, and I was kicking and screaming. In my obedience, I learned to hear God's voice more clearly. I began to discern not just His hand, but His heart. Sanctification silences the noise; it detached me from distraction. It taught me how to walk by faith and not by sight. It demanded absolute obedience.

I didn't realize how noisy my life had become until God led me into a place of stillness called consecration.

The silence wasn't empty; it was sacred. It echoed with His whispers. In isolation, I received revelation. When the voices of others faded, the voice of God grew even louder. In that place, I discovered I didn't need an audience; I needed an altar. And in the quiet, I learned the rhythm of heaven. Being set apart doesn't always feel holy at first. It feels like heartbreak, like abandonment, even like loss. Like endings you didn't expect and goodbyes you didn't rehearse. But hidden in the unraveling was an invitation to become. I was not being punished; I was being prepared. The breaking wasn't meant to destroy me, but to deliver me. I was shedding the old skin of who I thought I had to be to grow into who I was always meant to be.

Trials on Purpose

There were nights I cried in silence and mornings when I questioned if I had made a mistake. Loneliness can feel so loud when your surroundings fall silent. Over time, that ache transformed into an altar, and my tears nurtured seeds I didn't know I was planting. Slowly, gently, and painfully, beauty began to emerge from beneath the soil of surrender and trust.

I now understand that God sets you apart not just so you can see Him more clearly, but so others can see Him through you. Sanctification isn't about escaping the world; it's about becoming a light in it, and that light doesn't come from striving; it comes from staying. You might ask what I mean by staying: staying yielded, staying hidden, and staying close enough to the flame until His fire refines every part of your being. Separation wasn't just physical for me; it was internal. God wasn't only removing me from my people; He was breaking and removing generational patterns, mindsets, and dependencies. He was pruning away the places I hid, the excuses I made, and the lies I believed. It wasn't merely a relocation; it was a redefining. Not all pain stems from punishment; sometimes it's a sign that God is extracting something from you that can't accompany you to where He's leading. I had to set aside my pride, my need for understanding, and my craving for comfort. In the discomfort, amid the misunderstandings, I ultimately grew desperate not for answers, but for Him.

There's a peculiar kind of grief that comes with growth. A sorrow for sometimes reverting back to the old version of yourself, the one who survived but never truly lived. The one who performed but never truly rested, the one who loved others better than she loved herself. I had to mourn her, grieve her, understand her, bless her, and then bury her. Resurrection always follows surrender. In this grieving place, I discovered the difference between isolation and intimacy. One was a trick of the enemy; the other was a gift from God. When He sets you apart, it's never to punish you; it's always to purify. I wasn't forgotten when the enemy tried to whisper these thoughts in my mind. I was actually being focused; I wasn't abandoned; I was being purified and anointed. Somewhere in the hidden place, between the heartbreak and the healing, I began to see. I began to see that my tears were prayers when my mouth couldn't speak. That my wilderness was not punishment; it was the proving ground of my promise. That the pit was not a tomb but a womb that was birthing something beautiful, something great, something eternal.

Trials on Purpose

Chapter Three: Humbled for Glory

"God resists the proud but gives grace to the humble." (James 4:6)

Trials on Purpose

Trials on Purpose

Pride is a thief. It whispers self-sufficiency when your soul is starving for surrender. I used to believe humility was a weakness until life humbled me. Until grief, failure, disappointments, and uncertainty brought me low enough to look up. I learned that humility is thinking of yourself less so you can think of God more. When I finally let go of pleasing people and stopped needing applause to feel accepted and anointed, I discovered the beauty of hiddenness and the power of a heart fully surrendered, even when no one is watching. Trials strip us of false identities, and they unravel ego. They return us to the feet of Jesus, and it's there we remember who we are: not performers, not perfect, just His.

Pride doesn't just sit quietly; it craves praise. It feeds off applause, growing like a weed when nourished by the words of others. Before long, you start to believe the lie that, I made this happen. I built this life. I earned it. Pride will have you reaching for God's glory as if it were yours to claim. Exodus 20:5 reminds us that God is a jealous God. He does not share His glory. Think about how often we hear, I got that job because of *my* education, or, I got the part because I knew him or her. Those may be facts, but they aren't the full truth. Behind every open door and every opportunity, there is a divine appointment. It was God who aligned you with favor; it was His hand that opened the door that no man could shut.

Deuteronomy 8:2 declares, *"And you shall remember that the Lord your God led you all the way these forty years in the wilderness, to humble you and to test you, to know what was in your heart, whether you would keep His commandments or not."*

Trials on Purpose

God led the Israelites into the wilderness intentionally; He didn't lose track of them; He positioned them. Why? To humble them, to test them, and to reveal what was truly in their hearts. That sounds familiar, doesn't it? Maybe you've been in that place called wilderness. Perhaps you're there now, pushed out of your comfort zone, living in a state of complete dependence on God. In this place, it is not easy, but it is necessary. Testing isn't punishment; it's preparation. God sits high, watching not with cruelty but with anticipation: Will you apply what you learned in the last season to this one? Will you respond differently this time? The tests and trials are not designed to break you, but to shape you, to make survivors into soldiers, and weeping warriors into walking revivalists.

I've walked through seasons that brought me to my knees. I had to stop relying on my own strength and lean wholly on God. Sometimes, that moment only comes when you hit rock bottom, when every crutch is gone and every safety net is pulled away. It's in that low place where God whispers, "Now I can work." That's where compassion is born and where empathy begins to blossom. You stop judging and start listening. You begin to love differently, purely, and unconditionally. In that place, there's a paradigm shift in your thinking, speaking, perspective, and interactions. You stop reacting and start discerning.

Here's the truth: in your lowest moment, the enemy will try to highlight everything that's going wrong. He will emphasize what you have lost, what you've been through, and who walked away. But know that it's not the end of your story. It's in this vulnerable place that many make poor decisions, retreat back to old comforts, and fall into familiar habits. This is where you realize you have to retake the same test because you missed the lesson. That's when frustration sets in, not just with the process but also with God and ourselves. I really need you to catch this: the very fact that you're being tested means you're being trusted. God is trusting you with that trial; it's evidence He is calling you higher.

Ephesians 6 declares, *"Put on the whole armor of God that you may be able to stand against the wiles of the devil."* That sounds like a command to me: to stand and not retreat. Not to panic, but to stand. In this place, God strips away the deadly distractions. The people you thought would suddenly be there are gone. The calls you make go unanswered. The support you once had has fallen silent. Because God wants your full, undivided attention, He's after your intimacy. Yes, you may feel alone, but you're not abandoned.

If you're in Lodabar, a low place, a dry place, a confused or broken place, this is your call to rise. Wash your face and speak life over yourself. Say it out loud: **I'm coming out of this! I am an overcomer! I am redeemed! God has better for me!** Keep saying it until you begin to believe it. Isaiah 43:18–19 declares, *"Forget the former things… Behold, I will do a new thing! Now it springs forth, shall you not know it? I will make a way in the wilderness and rivers in the desert."*

You may not be where you want to be, but you're not forgotten. Stop comparing your journey to others; you don't know the price they paid for the oil in their lives. Stay focused on your process. That's the key: process. A process is a series of actions or steps taken to achieve a desired end. Isaiah 46:10 says, *"Declaring the end from the beginning…saying, My counsel shall stand, and I will do all My pleasure."* So that means your end was settled before your trial ever began. Your victory was declared before the battle ever started.

Even though it feels like death, Psalm 23:4 reminds us, *"Yea, though I walk through the valley of the shadow of death, I will fear no evil, for You are with me; Your rod and Your staff, they comfort me."* Remember, it's just a shadow; it may feel like the end, but it isn't. God is walking with you. Deuteronomy 31:8 speaks this truth: *"The Lord Himself goes before you, He will never leave you nor forsake you."* You may have faced near-death moments physically, emotionally, psychologically, and even spiritually, but the Holy Spirit stepped in. You're still here because God isn't done with you.

You remember the story of Shadrach, Meshach, and Abednego. They didn't bow to the pressure, and when the furnace was turned up seven times hotter, the fire didn't consume them; God showed up in the flames. When they came out, they didn't even smell like smoke. That's what God does. He doesn't just bring you through; He covers you gracefully, so you don't even look like what you've been through. Let that fuel your faith! Every trial has a purpose; it serves as a platform for the Word to come alive. John 1:1 tells us that *"the Word was made flesh and dwelt among us."*

That's Jesus; He is the Word. In your trial, He is becoming alive in you. You must yield to the process and be willing to say yes to it. The longer you resist, the longer it takes. Remember this: seeds grow in dirt, and the watering of the Word causes them to flourish. That dirt, which consists of your trials, discomforts, setbacks, storms, and pains, contains some of the seeds needed for growth. And when you water that dirt with the Word, the fruit of the Spirit begins to manifest wisdom, maturity, joy, peace, patience, love, and an undeniable anointing. I challenge you to choose humility; choose surrender.

1 Peter 5:6 says, *"Humble yourselves under the mighty hand of God, that He may exalt you in due time."* Ask yourself: *Will I humble myself, or will God have to do it for me? I will encourage you to choose to humble yourself, it will save you some heartache.*

If you're ready to let go of pride and fully surrender, pray this with me:

> Father, in the name of Jesus, I repent of my sins and forgive those who've sinned against me. I renounce the spirit of pride and every spirit tied to it. I close every door the enemy has used to access my life, and I seal it by the Blood of

Jesus. Satan, take your hands off me! I release the fire of God to burn away everything in me that's not like You. I receive a humble and contrite spirit. Restore to me the years the locust, the cankerworm, the palmerworm, and the caterpillar have stolen. I declare my freedom, my healing, and my breakthrough now by faith, in Jesus' name. Amen.

Now, if you've prayed that, give God praise right where you are! Your breakthrough is here. Your victory is real. Your process has a purpose. The only way left is up from here.

Chapter Four: The Posture of Prayer: Accessing Divine Power in the Midst of Trials

"Pray without ceasing." (1 Thessalonians 5:17)

Trials on Purpose

Trials on Purpose

Another vital purpose of trials is that they bring us into a posture of prayer.

In every relationship, communication is foundational, and this holds true for our relationship with God as well. Without prayer, our connection with the Father becomes distant and strained. Prayer is not just talking to God; it's an ongoing engagement in a divine dialogue. It involves both surrender and reception as our spirit communes with His.

Prayer acknowledges the reality and sovereignty of God. It serves as our access point to the throne room of grace. The Apostle Paul exhorts us in Philippians 4:6, *"Be anxious for nothing, but in everything by prayer and supplication, with thanksgiving, let your requests be made known to God."* The following verse continues, *"And the peace of God, which surpasses all understanding, will guard your hearts and minds through Christ Jesus."* These words are not just comforting; they are empowering. They remind us that peace is not circumstantial; it is supernatural, and it flows from divine communion and divine intimacy. God invites us to relinquish our burdens not with indifference or carelessness, but with complete trust in Him. To cast our cares is not to abandon responsibility but to surrender control. It is to say, Father, I trust Your will above my understanding. Our chief pursuit, then, is not resolution but alignment, pleasing the Father above all else.

We were created for worship, prayer, and praise. As we dedicate ourselves to His work, God commits Himself to ours. He is not an indifferent bystander to our needs; He is an attentive and good Father. Philippians 4:19 assures us, *"My God shall supply all your need according to His riches in glory by Christ Jesus."*

The questions we must often ask ourselves is:

Am I aligned with His will?

Am I in a position to hear and respond to His instructions?

Or am I merely presenting Him with my list of needs without making room for His voice?

So many of us pray yet walk away still carrying the weight of what we claimed to surrender. We place our burdens at the altar, only to retrieve them moments later and try to solve them in our own strength. To do this is to tie the hands of God. We crown ourselves as the deities over our own dilemmas, and in doing so, we welcome anxiety, doubt, fear, and unbelief, inviting torment where there should be peace.

There are seasons when God allows silence to surround us, and no solutions can be found. This is where He calls us, inviting us back to the posture of prayer. His still small voice whispers, *"Come to me, my child, I've already paved the way. Come commune with Me, and I will order your steps.* This is not just poetic; it is transformative. Prayer is the soil where divine transformation takes root. It is the space where sanity is preserved, wisdom is granted, and decisions are shaped by divine insight. Like a device disconnected from its power source, we can function for a while on spiritual residue, but eventually, depletion sets in.

Prayer is our fuel to recharge because God is our source. Staying connected through prayer doesn't just preserve us; it empowers us. In that sacred connection, He reveals hidden darkness, grants supernatural strength, supernatural access, and provides discernment. Prayer plugs us into the very mind of God; without it, nothing of eternal value can be birthed in the earth realm.

In *Genesis 1:27–28, we are reminded of our original mandate to have dominion, multiply, and subdue the earth.* That authority is still ours but is exercised through spiritual alignment. Through prayer, we realign ourselves with heaven's agenda and tune into God's voice. *"My sheep hear my voice, and I know them, and they follow me:" Jesus said in John 10:27. The key to knowing His voice is through communion and continual, unceasing prayer (1 Thessalonians 5:17).*

Prayer connects us to God's attribute of sovereignty. Nothing that happens in our lives escapes His notice. Not all trials are sent by God, but every trial is used by Him. God is so good that, in His supreme power, He weaves even our worst choices into a tapestry of redemption. There is always a consequence or reward attached to our decisions, but even in failure, God is faithful to deliver when we remain connected to Him.

The enemy's strategy is to divert our attention from God's promises and fix our eyes on our problems. He pulls us into the soulish realm, a domain governed by intellect, will, emotions, and past experiences. In this realm, we are reactionary, vulnerable, and fragile. Our belief systems, desires, thought processes, and emotional responses become the compass. But God is calling us higher. We must not settle for operating in our natural senses. The Spirit-led life demands that we detach from soulish distractions and realign with God's truth. In the soulish realm, the enemy sow's frustration, condemnation, doubt, and rebellion. But in the Spirit, God offers clarity, conviction, and power. That is why *Numbers 23:19* assures us that *"God is not a man, that He should lie."* Isaiah also lets us know that *"so shall my word be that goes forth out of my mouth: it shall not return unto me void, but it shall accomplish that which I please, and it shall prosper in the thing whereto I sent it."* (Isaiah 55:11).

We often forget just how faithful our God is. His goodness is not merely a theological statement; it is a lived reality. His word over your life is irrevocable, even if your steps have wandered. His plan is still in motion. That is why prayer is non-negotiable. We must continually seek downloads from heaven for fresh instruction that serves as our daily bread and divine direction. When God spoke to Jeremiah in chapter 1, verse 5, He made it clear: "Before I formed you in the womb, I knew you." That word still echoes in me and hopefully in every believer today. You are intentionally crafted, anointed, and appointed. God foreknew each misstep, every heartache, every detour, and every betrayal, and still chose you. Wow! Let that sink in for a moment! He infused you with grace, provision, and purpose.

When trials come, you should run to Him, not from Him. He's already provided a way of escape. I know what it means to walk through dark valleys. I have faced betrayal, heartbreak, abuse, loneliness, trauma, grief, divorce, mishaps, homelessness, and despair. I've felt the sting of failure and the weight of rejection. At times, I questioned whether I'd make it out. But in those lowest moments, God breathed life back into me. His still, small voice reminded me: *"You are more than a conqueror. You are the head and not the tail. You are chosen. You are mine."* Those declarations weren't just words; they were resurrection power. Strength returned, and determination ignited. And like the man at the pool of Bethesda, I picked up my bed and walked. I chose to leave the pity behind and pursue purpose with boldness. Every trial strips us of what is not eternal: old mindsets, toxic beliefs, pride, shame, and pain. You might ask yourself, why? So He can reveal who we truly are in Him, our true identity. This is where the paradigm shifts. In the fire, God refines; He replaces immaturity with wisdom and replaces reaction with revelation. The ultimate purpose is to align our agendas with heaven's mandate.

This is the purpose of the process: to mature and realign us, to recalibrate our souls. It aims to shift our source of guidance from intellect to revelation. With that revelation, we re-enter the world not just to survive but to lead. I suggest we return to the trenches, not as victims but as vessels. Yet many resist this process due to their unwillingness to wait. In an age of instant gratification, we have lost the art of patience. We resist authority, ignore spiritual discipline, and craft blueprints for our lives without consulting the great architect. By doing so, we open the door to the enemy's counterfeit promises. The enemy never shows you the price, only the bait. But the Word reminds us in Galatians 5:16, *"Walk in the Spirit, and you will not fulfill the lust of the flesh."*

Even in our failures, God's mercy meets us. He allows trials not to destroy us but to reintroduce us to His will. He reminds us of who we are and reaffirms what He has spoken. When we focus on the chaos around us, we become distracted, bitter, and disillusioned. The Holy Spirit's voice grows faint, our joy is stolen for a moment, and at other times for years. It all depends on how long we take to surrender again. When the trial comes, trust should be non-negotiable. I know this truth intimately.

Trials on Purpose

Even in moments when I questioned my worth and tried to end my life, Grace intervened. God breathed strength into my broken spirit. His voice thundered within, *"You are chosen, beloved, victorious, called, anointed, and mine."* From that sacred place, purpose emerged. My trials became testimonies. My pain became a platform to minister to someone else. I realized that God was not just rescuing me; He was reforming and redefining me. He stripped me of limited belief systems to usher me into a realm of revelation. This is what trials are meant to do, not to destroy, but to unveil. They peel back the layers of shame, guilt, bitterness, pride, and pain until all that remains is surrender. In that sacred space, a paradigm shift occurs. We exchange human reasoning for divine revelation. We cease planning our own agendas and begin seeking God's. When we surrender to this process, we become conduits of transformation. We then return to the battlefield of life, not merely to survive, but to pull others through. We become salt and light. We expand the Kingdom.

Nevertheless, many resist the process out of impatience and rebellion. We want the promise without undergoing the process. However, God's will cannot be bypassed. When we rely solely on our senses, what we see, feel, and desire we remain earthbound and spiritually stagnant. Ultimately, every distraction is meant to rob us of our joy, delay our destiny, and dull our spiritual sensitivity. Yet God, in His faithfulness, patiently waits for our hearts to yield; once we do yield, transformation begins.

Chapter Five: A People of Purpose

"Who hath saved us, and called us with an holy calling, not according to our works, but according to his own purpose and grace, which was given us in Christ Jesus before the world began," (2 Timothy 1:9)

Trials on Purpose

Trials on Purpose

God had already written your purpose before clocks or calendars ever measured time. You are not an outcast; you are not a mistake. You are the intentional breath of God, formed with precision and woven together with destiny in mind.

We often forget that we are created in the image of His Majesty. We forget that we are set apart, not for popularity or platforms, but for purpose. Somewhere between disappointment and delay, we have settled. We have diminished divine assignments to mere survival. We start to live like wanderers, not warriors; like orphans, not heirs. Yet the truth resonates louder than our circumstances: you were created to carry glory. There's a reason the enemy attacks you with such ferocity; it's not because of where you have been but because of where you're headed. The calling on your life terrifies hell. The enemy doesn't pursue the empty; he comes for the anointed. He seeks the one who carries a solution, a voice, and a mantle. You were born for impact.

You were born to break cycles of abuse, addiction, poverty, and silence. You were called to stand in the gap between heaven and earth, to declare, *"As for me and my house, we will serve the Lord." (Joshua 24:15)* The very fact that you're still breathing is evidence that God is not finished. No trauma, betrayal, setback, or failure has disqualified you. If anything, it has qualified you. It has given you oil. And oil only comes through the crushing. God doesn't waste pain; He recycles it into power. He saw it all every sleepless night, shattered dream, and whispered prayer that seemed to vanish into the void. He bottled every tear. You are not overlooked or forgotten; you are marked, chosen, and called. You are a people of purpose. But purpose doesn't always arrive wrapped in clarity. Sometimes it arrives cloaked in chaos. It appears as loss, rejection, shame, disappointment, or the lingering ache of waiting. Often, we think we've missed it. We assume we've strayed too far, waited too long, or wandered too much. But purpose doesn't expire due to detours. God doesn't discard the blueprint just because life has broken you. He uses the broken pieces to build something more beautiful than you could have imagined. What feels like a delay is often divine preparation. He's not just taking you somewhere; He's making and molding you into someone who will emerge as pure gold.

You may feel as if your story has chapters written in ink that you wish you could erase. But God is the Author who doesn't write people off; He writes people in and weaves redemption into every line and every story. He takes your shattered sentences and transforms them into sacred testimonies. The world needs your voice, not the polished version, but the real version. The voice that has journeyed through the valley and returned with oil. The voice that doesn't pretend it didn't bleed. There is a unique anointing on your life, not *de*spite your wounds, but because of them. You are not just surviving; you carry seeds of revival. Your life is not meant to blend in but to set others free. You are not a background character in the Kingdom; you are part of God's rescue plan for someone else. When you rise, others will rise. When you say yes, chains will begin to break that you may never see. When you choose healing, hope enters a bloodline that has never known it. You are the hinge point for future generations. You are not just here for a reason; I will tell you that you *are* the reason, light that enters dark places. Hold your head high, not in pride, but in remembrance. Heaven backed you even before anyone believed in you. Your name was spoken in eternity before you ever breathed. You are not too late, too broken, too excessive, or too far gone. You are right on time; the world doesn't need a perfect you, it needs a purposeful you. A heart surrendered, a spirit awakened. A life fueled by the flame of the refiner's fire. You are a people of purpose, and hell trembles because you're beginning to believe it.

Pray this prayer with me:

Father, sometimes I forget who I am. I forget what You whispered over me when the world was still formless and void. I forget that I was made with intention, not by accident. Father, forgive me for all the times I settled for less than what You had for me. Forgive me for listening to voices that told me I was too broken, too late, too flawed to matter. But today, I come in agreement with the truth Father, that I am chosen, called, peculiar, royal, and set apart. That I carry answers to prayers someone else is still praying, and I was born with a purpose. I surrender the weight of comparison and the sting of delay. I lay down shame, silence, and survival, and I pick up my mantle. Even in times when I feel forgotten, help me trust that You never miss a moment. You see every tear, you hear every silent prayer, and you collect every shattered piece, and somehow, you are still writing purpose on it all. Anoint me to walk boldly in what You've assigned to me. Even when I feel unqualified, remind me that you do not call the flawless, you call the surrendered. Let the oil from my crushing flow into the places where others are still bleeding. Use my pain for someone else's healing. Use my voice to call others into freedom. When the darkness tries to make me forget again, whisper this truth into my soul:

I am not an outcast, I am not forgotten. I am a person of purpose.

In Jesus' name,

Amen.

Chapter Six: The Process

"Trust in the Lord with all thine heart; and lean not unto thine own understanding." (Proverbs 3:5)

Trials on Purpose

Trials on Purpose

Purpose is never microwaved. It's marinated in the fire of process. The process... oh, the process... is far from glamorous. It involves breaking, undoing, and stripping away everything that is not like Him. It is where pride dies, and faith is born. It is where comfort is replaced by conviction. It is the hallway between who you were and who you are becoming. And it's in this in-between that God does His deepest work. We cry for the promise, but are we willing to endure the process?

The wilderness is not punishment; it is preparation. It is where idols are revealed, false identities are dismantled, and the flesh is crucified. It's the place where our 'yes' is tested and where our will collides with His. *Isaiah 43:18-19 declares, "Do not remember the former things; neither consider the things of old. Behold, I will do a new thing, and now it shall spring forth. Shall you not know it? I will even make a way in the wilderness and rivers in the desert."* God is forever moving and shifting things in our lives. He is not after performance; He's after surrender. In the process, you will lose people, lose possessions, lose platforms, and sometimes even lose yourself. Only then can you discover who you are in Him. You will be misunderstood, rejected, abandoned, and isolated. But take heart; so was Jesus. Like Jesus, we are called to take up our cross and follow, not out of convenience but out of covenant. God will never elevate what He cannot trust. He refines in obscurity; He tests in silence. He waits to see if we will obey without applause, if we will worship without a breakthrough, and if we will stay faithful without recognition. He's watching to see if your worship is tethered to who He is, not what He gives. He's checking if your faith can hold when everything around you is falling apart. He's pruning so you can bear fruit that lasts.

In the stillness of the process, God peels back the layers we've used to perform, to protect, to pretend. He touches the wounds we buried and the lies we believed. He exposes every cracked foundation, not to shame us, but to heal us. He will allow the shaking so that what's unshakable can remain. Not every closed door is rejection. Sometimes it's redirection; sometimes it's because you're not who you need to be yet to walk through it; you are not ready at the time. Resurrection always follows death. What's dying within you is making room for what's divine. God is preparing a vessel that can carry the weight of His glory without leaking or compromise. He's cultivating a heart that won't take credit for what only grace can build. He's building your soul; He's building up the whole you.

Trials on Purpose

If you're in the furnace, if life feels like one long night, don't despair. You're not being buried; you're not being burned; you're being planted. And what's planted in tears will bloom in power. The process isn't punishment; it's proof. Proof that there's oil on your life, proof that you're called for more. Let the fire refine you, let the waiting mold you, and let the breaking usher in the birthing. Because when God finally unveils what He's been doing in the dark, it will be nothing short of glory. When we pass the test and remain planted, postured, and prayerful, He releases the promise. Don't rush the process. Don't curse it. Embrace it. It's not killing you; it's revealing you.

Chapter Seven: The War You Didn't See Coming

"For the weapons of our warefare are not carnal, but mighty through God to the pulling down of the strong holds;"
(1 Corinthians 10:4)

Trials on Purpose

Trials on Purpose

The moment you said yes to Jesus, you were marked not only with glory but also with a target. The angels rejoiced, and hell took notice. This is not meant to make you afraid; it is intended to make you aware. Once you belong to Christ, the enemy will try everything to steal your joy, peace, and purpose. If he cannot destroy you, he will attempt to distract you. You need to know this: you are in a war. *Not a war of flesh and blood, but of principalities and powers, against the rulers of the darkness of this world, against spiritual wickedness in high places, lies, cycles, and atmospheres (Ephesians 6:12).*

This is spiritual, this is ancient, and this is very real. The fight isn't always loud; sometimes it is the quiet discouragement that creeps in at midnight. The anxiety that tightens your chest before an assignment. The sudden apathy about things you used to be passionate about, and the old temptations dressed in new faces. Believe me, that's not random. That is war! But here's the truth: hell doesn't want you to know you're not powerless; you've been given weapons. Heaven-forged, Spirit-saturated, unstoppable weapons. You are fully loaded.

Below you will find some of the most powerful weapons!

- ***The Word of God: sharper than any sword, able to silence every lie.***
- ***The blood of Jesus: the eternal proof that the devil already lost.***
- ***The name of Jesus: the authority above every other name.***
- ***The Holy Spirit: your Counselor, your Advocate, your Defender.***

- ***Worship : the sound that confuses the enemy and reminds your soul who God is.***

You don't fight for victory; you fight from the place of victory. But you must fight. You have to get up, wipe your tears, and put on the spiritual armor. Stop agreeing with the lies that say you're weak, tired, or not cut out for this. You were born for this battle, anointed for this hour, and trained in the fire. Every attack has a purpose, and every tear is being counted.

Every night you pressed through, Heaven was recording. God is not just watching you suffer; *He is training your hands for war and your fingers to fight (Psalm 144:1).*

You are not losing; you are learning. Remember that the enemy attacks what he fears, even when you feel like all hell is breaking loose.

Trials on Purpose

Chapter Eight: Warfare Isn't Proof God Left, It's Proof You're Advancing

"For I am persuaded, that neither death, nor life, nor angels, nor principalities, nor powers, nor things present, nor things to come, Nor height, nor depth, nor any other creature, shall be able to separate us from the love of God, which is in Christ Jesus our Lord." (Romans 8:38-39)

Trials on Purpose

Trials on Purpose

Some people mistake the intensity of spiritual warfare for God's absence. But that's a lie. The shaking doesn't mean God has stepped away; it means the ground beneath your feet is being reclaimed. Demonic systems are losing their grip, cycles are breaking, curses are being reversed, and chains are being shattered. You aren't facing more attacks because you backslid; you're facing more attacks because you're moving forward.

Warfare comes in waves, as destinies unfold in layers. Every time you say yes to the next level, you awaken resistance. But don't shrink back, don't second-guess yourself, and please don't run. The battle confirms the blessing; ask any soldier they don't get shot at for standing still. The bullets start flying when you move toward the objective. What you're feeling; the pressure, the confusion, the opposition, it's not because God left you. It's because you're becoming dangerous. You were once quiet and passive; then, you posed no threat. The enemy didn't need to bother you; your silence was agreement enough. Then something changed: you started waking up. You began praying differently. You stopped tolerating what used to enslave you. You deleted numbers, turned down the volume on culture, got rid of distractions, and started asking God for more, and hell noticed. You didn't just get attacked; you got marked.

Not with shame, but with the scent of oil. Listen to me: the enemy doesn't fight you because of your past. He fights you because of your future. He's not chasing who you used to be; he's terrified of who you're becoming. When the resistance increases, I challenge you to change your perspective.

Don't ask God, where are you? Ask God, what am I carrying that hell is trying to abort?

The next time trials arise, the next time voices whisper, the next time hell sends a familiar temptation dressed as comfort or a distraction, look it in the eye and say: You should've killed me when you had the chance. But now I know who I am. Every time the ground shakes beneath your feet, don't panic; you're not falling apart; you're breaking new ground. The tremors in your soul, the warfare in your mind, and the sudden emotional whirlwinds are not signs of divine abandonment. Instead, they indicate that strongholds are losing their grip. That generational curse of insecurity is trembling. That silent shame from abuse is cracking. That old addiction that thought it owned you is gasping for breath. You may think you're losing it, but you're not; you're being loosed. The shaking is uncomfortable because it's unfamiliar. But don't interpret the earthquake as punishment. It's deliverance; Heaven is moving on your behalf, and anything that can't stand in His presence must fall. This is about mantles, this is about assignments, this is about the souls connected to your obedience. You said yes to more, and that yes echoed in the spirit realm. Don't think that warfare means you made a wrong turn; it's confirmation that you're on the right path. Stay low, stay sharp, stay in prayer. Resistance increases right before release.

Chapter Nine: You Can't Walk in Public Authority Without Private Crushing

"That the trial of your faith, being much more precious than of gold that perisheth, though it be tried with fire, might be found unto praise and honour and glory at the appearing of Jesus Christ: (1 Peter 1:7)

Trials on Purpose

Trials on Purpose

Let's talk about the olive. It's small, ordinary-looking, and can be easily overlooked. However, what most people desire from the olive isn't its appearance or even its taste; it's the oil inside. That oil is healing, sacred, and valuable. But to obtain the oil, it must be crushed, pressed, beaten, and broken open. There's simply no other way. And family, it's the same with you. You've prayed for the anointing, asked God for purpose, and cried out for more of Him.

When the pressure mounted and life began to feel like a slow grind of pressure, pain, and tears, you wondered if you were being punished. You weren't; you were being prepared. The anointing doesn't come from the spotlight; it comes from surrender, from pressure, and from the nights when you couldn't breathe but still chose to praise

Him. Everyone wants to be used by God until they realize what it truly costs.

David was anointed in private long before he ever wore a crown. Between the oil and the throne lies betrayal, trials, wilderness, and waiting. A shallow vessel will leak under the weight of true authority because God loves you too much to give you influence without depth. He will refine you in the hidden place, using disappointment to teach you discernment and heartbreak to sharpen your hunger, teaching you how to guard your heart. He will allow you to walk through silence so that when you speak, demons tremble. You are not going through hell just to survive it; you are undergoing a process to emerge dripping with oil, the anointing. The oil that heals, the oil that frees, the oil that destroys yokes. You may not like where you are right now and may feel tired, frustrated, and confused.

I challenge you to stop cursing this season and start consecrating it.

Repeat this: **God, I don't understand this, but I give it to You. Lord, if this is what it takes to carry the oil, I surrender. Crucify what You must in me; purify what You will. I belong to You.**

Once you surrender to the crushing, the crushing becomes holy. Your tears become prayers, your groans become warfare, and your broken places become altars, and the oil starts to flow. You may feel like a shattered mess right now, but God sees oil. You may not recognize yourself in the mirror, but heaven recognizes the weight being formed in you. When this season is over, and it will end, you won't just come out surviving; you'll come out dripping with substance. Dripping with power, dripping with peace, dripping with compassion, dripping with discernment, dripping with anointing, and dripping with joy that the world didn't give and can't take away. When you speak, your words won't be empty; they will be anointed fire sent to do what they were created to do. Because the crushing didn't just break you; it built you. From this moment forward, the enemy will smell the oil's fragrance wherever you go.

When the trial comes, run to Him, not from Him. Trust becomes non-negotiable. I know this truth intimately. I have weathered being downtrodden, heartbreak, rejection, despair, and even moments when I questioned my worth and contemplated ending my life. But grace interrupted, and mercy intervened. God breathed strength into my broken spirit. His voice thundered within, "You are set apart, loved, peculiar, victorious, and mine." From that sacred place, purpose emerged. I realized that God was not just rescuing me; He was summoning me to a higher place in Him. This is what trials are meant to do: not to destroy, but to unveil. They peel back the layers of shame, bitterness, pride, trauma, generational labels, and pain until all that remains is surrender. In that sacred space, a paradigm shift occurs. We trade human reasoning for divine revelation. We stop planning our own agendas and start seeking God's will for our lives. When we surrender to this process, we become conduits of transformation. We return to the battlefield of life, not merely to survive, but to help pull others through. We become salt and light, expanding the Kingdom.

Nevertheless, many resist the process due to impatience, disobedience, and rebellion. We desire the promise without embracing the journey. However, God's will cannot be circumvented. When we rely solely on our senses, what we see, feel, hear, touch, and desire, we remain tethered to the earth and spiritually stagnant. The enemy takes advantage of this, offering us enticing counterfeits without revealing the true cost. But *Galatians 5:16* admonishes, *"Walk in the Spirit, and you will not fulfill the lust of the flesh."* Even in our disobedience, God, rich in mercy, permits trials to redirect us, reintroduce His will, and redefine our identity in Him. Every distraction is designed to rob us of our joy, delay our destiny, and dull our spiritual sensitivity. Yet, God, in His faithfulness, patiently waits for our hearts to yield. Once we yield to Him, transformation begins.

Chapter Ten: The Restoration

"Therefore if any man be in Christ, he is a new creature: old things are passed away; behold, all things are become new." (2 Corinthians 5:17)

Trials on Purpose

Trials on Purpose

God doesn't just save you; He also restores you. Salvation is the beginning, while restoration is the healing, the mending, and the unbreaking. It's the quiet miracle that unfolds in the months after your "yes." When the applause fades and the lights go out, when it's just you, your wounds, and the whisper of God. The world teaches us to cover what's cracked, but the Kingdom invites us to uncover it so glory can pour through the gaps. God never asked you to be perfect; He only asked you to be real. Real is where the healing happens. Let God into the rooms you've kept locked for years, into the trauma you've tried to outgrow, into the night you wish never happened, and into the guilt you've worn like skin. Let Him into the childhood memories you swore you buried, the relationship that shattered your ability to trust, and the shame that clings like smoke after a fire. Let God into the closet where the skeletons still rattle when no one's around. He doesn't flinch. He doesn't recoil. The very thing you think disqualifies you is what God wants to redeem. He doesn't just forgive sin; He restores identity. He won't just heal the wound; He will redefine the scar. You are not too far gone; you are not too broken. If you give Him the ashes, He will give you beauty. If you give Him the mess, He will give you a ministry. You're not a second-class citizen in the Kingdom. You're a son; you're a daughter. You are being restored, not to who you used to be, but to who you were always meant to be. Restoration is not the erasure of pain; it's the repurposing of it. He uses what you experienced to heal others. Your scars will speak, and your tears will teach. Your journey will become someone else's roadmap. So, stay in His hands. Restoration takes time, but it's worth every moment. There's oil in the process, and there's glory in the ruins. He is rebuilding you. God says, *"I will restore to you the years that the swarming locust has eaten"* (Joel 2:25).

When God finishes rebuilding you, you won't resemble what you've endured. You'll resemble Him. You've worn names that didn't belong to you for long enough, names like failure, too much, not enough, unworthy, forgotten, and damaged goods. Today, Heaven reminds you that these are not your names. Your identity was spoken before the foundations of the world, before the heartbreak, before the rejection, before the trauma, and before religion misrepresented Him. God already knew you. The world tried to rename you based on your trauma, but God names you based on your truth. You are not the divorce, you are not the addiction, you are not the secret sin, the bankruptcy, or the night you lost control. You are not your past or even what you did an hour ago. You are His; you are chosen, made whole, righteous, redeemed, worthy, loved, a royal priesthood, a holy nation, set apart and sealed by His Spirit. He wrote your name in the Book of Life, not in pencil or pen but in His blood. It's time to agree with Heaven, not just in theory but in identity. When you know who you are, the devil loses his grip. You don't have to strive to be enough; you are already enough. You don't have to chase man's approval; you are already loved. You don't have to fear being unseen; the God who knows the number of hairs on your head has never taken His eyes off you. Let shame fall. Let the old names drop; you are not who they said you were. You are who He says you are, and that changes everything. This is restoration, not just a return but a resurrection. You're coming back brighter, bolder, stronger, whole, and full of wisdom. When God is finished, I promise, you will not look like what you've been through, and you will not even smell like smoke.

Readers Reflection

Take a moment and breathe deeply. You've made it to the end of these pages, but in so many ways, this isn't an ending at all. It's a beginning, a threshold, a sacred invitation into wholeness. You didn't just read a book; you journeyed through wisdom, intentional healing, and deliverance. You sat in rooms you once kept locked. You confronted wounds you thought were too old to name. And somehow, God met you in every chapter with kindness that didn't shame you and truth that didn't crush you. You may not have even realized it until now, but restoration has already begun. You might have cried, not just sad tears, but sacred ones that led to something breaking so that something else could begin. The kind that tells Heaven: I'm ready now, I do not want to hide anymore. Those are tears wrapped in oil; your story is an altar, and this moment is holy ground. Maybe you realize that you are not alone in your pain for the first time. You are not lost in your process; your past does not disqualify you. You are deeply, irrevocably loved. *"The Lord is close to the brokenhearted and saves those who are crushed in spirit." (Psalm 34:18).*

Before you close this book, I invite you to do one thing: look back at your own life with holy eyes. Not eyes of shame, not eyes of defeat, not eyes of what could've been, but eyes that see the fingerprints of God even in the dark. Eyes that recognize that I didn't die there; I didn't stay stuck there; I made it through that. If I made it through that, there must be glory on the other side. This trial is definitely on purpose! The fact that you're still breathing proves there's more to come. Not just survival, but restoration, not just healing, but purpose; not just forgiveness, but full redemption.

You don't have to prove anything to God. You simply need to give Him your Yes. A trembling yes, a God, I don't know how, but I trust You kind of yes. He's not after your perfection. He's after your permission. Let Him finish what He started. Let Him rebuild you, not back into who you used to be, but into who you were always meant to become. You are chosen! You are called! You are set apart! You are a royal priesthood! You are loved! You are His!

Trials on Purpose

Trials on Purpose
50 Affirmations for your Soul

- I Am aware of God's presence, even in my pain.

- I Am never alone; God is always with me.

- I Am led by a divine purpose greater than my understanding.

- I Am tuned in to God's voice, even in His silence.

- I Am able to see God's fingerprints in every season of my life.

- I Am not what I've been through; I am who God says I am.

- I Am more than my circumstances.

- I Am victorious because God fights for me.

- I Am empowered to rise above adversity.

- I Am moving from survival to thriving in Christ.

- I Am filled with the Holy Spirit.

Trials on Purpose

- I Am resilient because God is my source.

- I Am standing firm with supernatural courage.

- I Am renewed daily by God's mercy and grace.

- I Am unshaken, for the Spirit within me is greater than what's around me.

- I Am not being punished I am being prepared.

- I Am embracing pain as a tool, not a torment.

- I Am learning through the fire, not lost in it.

- I Am shaped, not shattered, by trials.

- I Am walking in my purpose, even when it hurts.

- I Am growing wiser with each test.

- I Am coming out stronger than I went in.

- I Am closer to God now than I've ever been.

- I Am transformed by the renewing of my mind.

- I Am being refined for God's glory.

- I Am courageous in the face of uncertainty.

- I Am walking in clarity because God orders my steps.

- I Am anchored in unshakeable faith.

- I Am trusting God even when I don't understand.

- I Am confident that my story is still unfolding.

- I Am living on purpose, not by accident.

- I Am aligned with Heaven's assignment for my life.

- I Am equipped for every trial I face.

- I Am a vessel of God's glory through my story.

- I Am advancing, not retreating.

- I Am chosen and set apart by God.

- I Am healed, whole, and holy in Him.

- I Am proof that pain has a purpose.

- I Am a living testimony of God's grace.

- I Am not finished God is still writing my story.

- I Am enduring with patience because I know God is at work.

- I Am rooted in faith that outlasts the storm.

- I Am becoming who God created me to be, through the process, not in spite of it.

- I Am learning to praise God in the middle of the trial.

- I Am free from fear because perfect love casts it out.

- I Am not broken; I am being built.

- I Am a warrior clothed in God's strength.

- I Am rising from the ashes with purpose and power.

- I Am walking out of the wilderness with wisdom.

- ***I AM THE EVIDENCE THAT GOD CAN TURN PAIN INTO PURPOSE!***

Trials on Purpose

Final Prayers: God, Use My Trials for Your Glory

Father,

I come to You, not with eloquence of speech but with honesty, not with answers, but with surrender, you see the whole story. You see every tear before it falls, you hear the cries I never spoke out loud. And still, You have never left, thank You for not wasting any of my trials. Not the heartbreak, not the failure, not the seasons I thought would kill me. Not the nights I didn't know if I would make it to morning. You saw purpose in what looked like pain. You saw destiny wrapped in the dust. You saw me, not for what I did, but for who. You made me to be. God, I give You every trial, every scar, every storm, every shattered piece. Make something eternal from it. If it broke me, let it birth something holy. If it crushed me, let it carry oil. If it costs me everything, let it make me more like You. Restore what was lost, resurrect what died, redeem what was stolen.

I release every false name I've carried.

I reject every lie of the enemy,

Today, I choose to believe what You've spoken:

That I am loved.

That I am chosen.

That I am Yours.

That I am worthy.

That I am more than a conqueror.

That I can do all things through Christ that strengthens me.

Write purpose into my pain.

Breathe life into what I buried.

And when the world sees me, let them see Your fingerprints all over my story.

Not perfect, but restored.

Not famous, but faithful.

Not without scars, but sealed with grace.

Let my life be proof that even trials have a purpose.

In Jesus holy and matchless name

Amen.

Trials on Purpose

Trials on Purpose
Prayer of Salvation

If you've read this far, it's not by accident. The Spirit of God is tugging at your heart, not to shame, but to save. Not to condemn, but to call you amongst the family. Perhaps you've wandered, perhaps you've been wounded by life, family, religion, or even yourself. But the Father is waiting with open arms and fierce love. No matter how far you've gone, grace goes farther. He's not asking for perfection. He's asking for surrender. If you're ready to begin again… if you're ready to exchange brokenness for belonging, sin for salvation, pain for purpose, then pray this prayer with me:

> Father, I come before you broken, lost, hurt, and in need of a Savior. I believe Jesus Christ is Your Son, that He died for my sins, and rose again in power. I confess my need for You,

wash me, forgive me and restore me. I surrender my life into Your hands. Be my Lord, be my King. From this day forward, I belong to You. In Jesus' name. Amen.

If you prayed that prayer, welcome home. Heaven is rejoicing, and so am I. This is not the end, but it is the glorious beginning. God is rewriting your story. And what's coming will be greater than what's been. Please reach out to my team and I, we would love to connect with you.

ABOUT THE AUTHOR

Schniece M. Lambert is more than just a writer; she is a visionary. She carries a voice carved from the wilderness and deep in the valley, not only from the mountaintop. As a bearer of grace, scars, miracles, signs, and mercy, her wisdom and Divine Insight come from the trenches of transformation, where God's presence met pain, and the Word became a lifeline. Schniece bears a mantle and a passion to speak life into dry bones, to call prodigals home, to unmask shame with truth, and to ignite a generation to walk boldly in their God-given identity. With a heart rooted in love and the Word, and a voice seasoned by trial, Schniece writes for those who thought they were too far gone: the misfits, the forsaken, and the outcast; for those wrestling in silence, and for those who still have a flicker of faith beneath the ashes. Schniece has been blessed with many gifts and wears many hats, including Prophet, Minister, Realtor, Insurance Broker, Life Coach, Business Consultant, and CEO of The Redefined You, LLC. Schniece is a native of Paterson, NJ and currently resides in Virginia with her children and grandchildren. Stay in touch: visit www.theredefinedyou.net

Trials on Purpose

www.ingramcontent.com/pod-product-compliance
Lightning Source LLC
Chambersburg PA
CBHW050520100526
44581CB00001B/46